Cricket to Corporate

Kapil Pathare

PARTRIDGE
A Penguin Random House Company

To order additional copies of this book, contact
Partridge India
000 800 10062 62
orders.india@partridgepublishing.com

www.partridgepublishing.com/india

Kapil Pathare

At the initiation of 21st century, Maxwell Industries Ltd., a VIP Group Company, witnessed introduction of enthusiastic, young and dynamic leadership in the Board Of Directors. Mr. Kapil Jaykumar Pathare at a tender age of 21 engraved his name in the Company and impressed the whole with his situational leadership style, spot decision making abilities and as an effective communicator of management decisions. Since the beginning, he has been inclined more towards the operations side of the Management Functionary, besides other functions. He focused more on various aspects of Manufacturing of innerwear goods with his clear concept of quality of products & services. He always describes that Maxwell is a pioneer of innerwear manufacturers but moreover, we are innovating marketing Company. With this enthusiasm and customer oriented global vision, he has made a great difference in the then manufacturing & marketing traditions & styles. To be as a global innerwear manufacturer, he possess an absolute clear vision which is armed with right attitude and fundamental understanding of human being. He believes in success of business personnel depends on right understanding of human resources, their approaches, skills and values of those who work in the Organization.

Mr. Kapil Pathare did pursue his Masters in Business Administration after his Graduation in Commerce discipline and has equipped himself on professional front by undergoing various seminars, conferences and updating himself through the mentoring process. It will not be out of place to mention here that Mr. Pathare acquired fundamental skills and knowledge of business systems, procedures & technical aspects by being with the people on the floor and understanding the nitigrities thereof through the people in-charge of the operations. With this blend of vision and action he has been leading a team of professionals and setting up SMART (Specific, Measurable, Achievable, Realistic, Time bound) objectives for the team to achieve in the areas of manufacturing and marketing of innerwear, lingerie, readymade garments, socks and other accessories.

Maxwell Industries Ltd. is a name well versed with and affiliated to many fashion Awards for more than two decades, to name the few at its credit, ABBY's Gold 2005, Golden Scale Trophy (2007-2008) - The Brand of the year Women's Inner Wear By CMAI, Golden Scale Trophy (2007-2008) - The Brand of the year Men's Inner Wear By CMAI, Golden Scale Trophy (2006-2007) - The Brand of the year Men's Inner Wear By CMAI, IMA -Image Fashion Award, Lycra Fashion Award : Most Admired Innerwear Company of the year - VIP Group.

The Company has been continuously engaged in branding of products and emerging its image from masses brands to premium Brands. The Company's foresight in placing Frenchie and Frenchie X innerwear brands in Indian market and abroad have created a passion for innerwear in young generation of the Country. Recently, the Company also had tie-up with a French premium brand – Eminence, to manufacture and cater in the Indian market. Mr. Kapil Pathare is a consistent follower of Change Management thinking preceded with Kaizen and principle of Just-in-time in the areas of inventory management. He always states," Time Is The Essence Of The Management" and therefore he believes in timely delivery of the results for the development & prosperity of the Company.

Kapil also has a strategic tie up with events company for organizing various corporate and film events along with biking events. His passion for riding bike brings him meditation in life. Mr Kapil is a true cricket lover and loves to watch cricket even at times in stadiums and travel different parts of world to watch cricket.

COVER this book... **EXTRA COVER** it
Don't let the opportunity **SLIP**!
Available in a **GULLY** near your house
That's the **POINT** I am making
A **THIRD MAN** told you, it's a **SILLY POINT** is it?

Contents

Chapter 1   Early beginnings –
Child Prodigies all!. 1

Chapter 2   Gully Cricket 11

Chapter 3   Change Is The Only Constant!. 23

Chapter 4   Once Upon A Time... One Day.... 33

Chapter 5   Twenty Something! 43

Chapter 6   Indian Premier League 49

Chapter 7   Level Playing Field! 57

Chapter 8   Does Man At The Top Determine
The Team's Destiny? 73

Chapter 9   Positions & Positioning View. 83

Chapter 10 Cricket as a Theatrical
Performance On Stage! 91

Chapter 11 Cricket and Corporate. 99

Chapter 1

Early beginnings – Child Prodigies all!

As you roll the plastic ball on the ground without giving it any bounce, the child just blindly swings the bat and irrespective of the outcome – You shout -- Aaeee... Four! Aaeee..... Wow Sixer! Shotttt!

These are the three words we must be instilling in every child as he holds the plastic contraption called a Cricket Bat, and you bowl to this child during the early days.

Irrespective of the interest of the child, Cricket is a compulsory game that every child goes through, and is considered a Child Prodigy. This makes me wonder, while we have so many sports, why we don't give the child a big ball and play football with it, or why do we not teach it to run the professional way like an athlete, or better still, why don't we buy badminton rackets or table tennis bats for the child.

Most important of all, why don't we buy hockey stick toys and make the child play the game in whatever form we think fit. You may think this is all wishful thinking, but try and think deeper? What did your toy bag consist of – different models of toy cars, buses, airplane, jeeps, some toys that make noise on winding the key, a train set, and a cricket bat and ball.

No child's toy set is complete without this component.

What is even more amazing is the way all the children hold the bat. At about 60 degrees. The gap between the bat and pad is so wide, that the toy box of the child can be passed through that gap. Yet the first hope that the child is given that he or she is a prodigy and has managed to hit a four or six or a great shot.

With the evolution of this prodigy, correspondingly the density of plastic bat increase. Now the child has a plastic bat that is as firm as a stick, and a plastic ball that is harder. The child is now ready to step out of home and mingle with friends in the neighbourhood and take his first steps towards displaying his or her inborn talent, nurtured by the parent.

In this evolution, the degree also reduces and now the child has been able to achieve the conventional 0-5 degree tilt of the bat, and has started resembling a budding cricketer.

The prodigy now gets exposure to some real world scenarios, and the degree of skill emerges, because there is a comparison with other prodigies. Yet most of the children only want to bat first, nobody wants to bowl. Most of the child game fights or complaints are because of one person batting and then abandoning the game, and the other person who bowled now feels cheated that they did not get the batting and the game has been abandoned.

Such battles could result into mutually arbitrary disciplinary actions. One vowing to the other that I will never ever play cricket with you ever again, and the other not getting rattled by this threat.

Now the threat deepens – I will never play any game with you ever again, Video Games, Computer Games, Racer games, cycle and so on. The other party is still not perturbed over the threat and agrees. Now the threat get stronger --– I will never ever talk to you for all my life, and yet the other person says ok, as if he has not committed any crime of having denied batting to the other person.

But come evening or come tomorrow and the two have to get together, because they have no other person to play with. All those postures are like just plain dialogues that will get repeated in the course of their life till they mature. The game goes on, and today just to placate the other person who was the victim in the earlier scenario, gets to bat first. Now things are back to normal.

The cold war goes on amongst the prodigies – in terms of who get the bat, or who gets the ball. This is one of the most important element in the power politics that they get attuned to. If the one who has the bat and the ball get together, then they set the rules, else if they are in opposing teams, to every rule there is a counter rule and the either party threatening one another like coalition partners.

Such battles are interesting, and take the route of advanced conflict management that one learns in management. The way the game progresses with one team marginalized or some individuals marginalized, and some rule with aplomb.

Another funny thing to observe among these prodigies is their stake on claim to style. Every one like to say that they play like `Tendulkar' (first preference) and this is usually bestowed on the leader or the person who owns the bat. Bowling is a routine activity and not much importance attached to it. Remember the culture of "batting" being given more importance.

Idols beyond India are rarely chosen, and at this early age. The other idols are not beyond the first four or five enduring batsmen in the team. Left hand batsmen are detested at this level and never taken as idols. If you shape as a left hand batsman at this level, you are more a liability, and you have to adjust to be right handed batsmen.

Think about it. How many of you feel a bit shocked when your child first tries to take a stance as a left hand batsman. Some of us even get into correcting the stance of the child, and try make it right handed. No surprise that we tend to rarely see not more than 3 left hand batsmen in the National side.

So much of nuances behind a child that is trying to get initiated into not a game, but a religion of the country, or more so religion of South Asia – Cricket, wonder what would be the state of upbringing of children across other countries in the region, or the way children grow up in other cricket playing countries.

Would they be taking to cricket so early? Would there be so many child prodigies? Would a child have the luxury of having a coach and mentor at that tender age? Or is this a phenomenon only unique to India?

Some children may take to a different sport, but it is extremely embarrassing to say that you don't know how to play cricket. It would be interesting to find out about some Indian greats in other sports like boxing, shooting, Badminton, tennis, and Chess as to how did they grow up and when did the interest in such a sport come into them. What do they think of cricket?

The important in upbringing of the prodigies in India is that right from that early age the child learns to adapt to the circumstances. An entire match in whatever form is played in an area far lesser than 22 yards.

Stump or no stump, there are many makeshift stumps and there is an appeal for clean bowled and counter arguments that the ball may have missed the off-stump or have gone over the stump and so on.

The even more interesting scenes are to witness the comments of these prodigies. After a match the way they criticize the international players, the shots played, coach strategies, and tactics adopted would make a normal person feel as to from where and how have these budding expert commentators gathered such valuable insights from.

Who teaches them? How have they achieved the qualification of passing comments about the International players? The way these children are able to convert hearsay into conversation is extremely amazing.

We should drop the opener, or why was this person sent at this number and not promoted up the batting order, I don't know why the captain is persisting with this bowler, and who is the fastest bowler and this even extends to interesting trivia and tales that these prodigies would like to share as if they witnessed all these scenes directly.

Now cut to the corporate world and everyone is bought up with the thought that one would lead an enterprise one day, and right from childhood the seeds of ambitions are sown. Like the Aee Four! And Aee Six! And Shotttt!, the growing child is taught that he will lead a big enterprise and be as big as the TATAs, Birla's, Ambani's, Narayanamurthy's, Nilekani's, and Azim Premji's, etc.,

Depending on the track record at education that is given utmost importance, most have to shape up as studious and score high marks in academics to qualify for the best of class education, thus get into the best of college, and best of further education, and then the best of the company, and then start a business that is best of category.

Are we back to some wishful thinking? Yes and No, because, be it cricket or your career, all of us being as prodigies in our respective fields. Rich-Poor or Middle Class, all are equal when it comes to this quality, but the environment and exposure matters the most.

We know of tales of people who have not been so rich, but come up with great business ideas and become Industry captains, and similarly the recent phenomenon in the Indian team is also a clear reflection of the times with excellent talent from non metro cities, and towns emerging, and those players making a niche for themselves in the National side.

Some make it, some flounder on the way, but all of them know how to play. The important thing is all have an opinion on how the Professionals should play, and castigate them. In Life, we all start similar, but the spirit of enterprise differs, as this is dependent on the environment you grow in, what you make of it, and so on. Whether people get into business or not, everyone has an opinion on how you should run your business. No wonder someone coined the term "Mind Your Own Business"

Chapter 2

GULLY CRICKET

The child prodigies have now grown up. The area that they have been playing is now smaller, or the neighbours are objecting, or the shots these children play have been much stronger.

Life has also got boring playing the same opponent – some just 3-4 people. I bat, you bowl, no runner. That stage is soon getting to be very boring, and hence the need to transition to the next level has come.

The first level of merger happens – the opponents become the same team, and now the first phase of a bigger game happens, and a whole new game opens up. You now have a partner with whom you have to co-ordinate and score.

Understanding, rapport, synchronizing, body language, and a new sense of alertness comes out of this newly acquired status of the game, and the format. The field is a little larger, and the number of players have now increased to about four to six a side.

New hierarchies are drawn up, because one has to prove oneself completely afresh in this new scenario, though people like to talk about their past performances, and achievements. This is a totally new field, and obviously the performances here matter the most for one to deserve recognition.

Perhaps this is the place where some kind of skill realization dawns in, where the player begins to realize that he is better in batting, or some good in bowling, and some excel all-round.

This is also soon noticed in some specially acquired skills of some elegant strokes, some confident bowlers – essentially spinners. Pace bowling is strictly not allowed as most of the games are played underarm. There is no run up, just two steps, and you turn your arm. The ball will tend to cut or spin, and the batsmen then has the challenge of negotiating the same with all the guile and skill. Hence there is not a bowling style, it is a rudimentary action, and basis that a bowler is judged.

The rules are still arbitrary and those who own the bat or the ball, may get a chance to frame the rules of the game as per adaptations they would like for the game. Rest of the crowd surprisingly tends to cave in to such demands, seek minor clarifications and play on because life has to go on.

Amoebic Shapes-Adaptability

The most amazing thing about a cricket field in gully cricket is the shape. This depends on the field that gets inherited or found. Most of the fields are with a wall at the back and that serves as the stump, drawn with a piece of chalk, or scratched with a stone.

The layout may be such that there is minimal or no off side to the wicket. This impacts the bowlers, the batsmen and the fields set, for one has to become a natural onside player.

When the layout is such that there is minimal or no onside to the wicket, again the game takes a new turn, because players have to now adapt to a new field, and so do the bowlers.

There are times when the off or the onside has a good depth, but you cannot play the strokes on those sides because – either the person staying on the ground floor is objecting to your playing, or there are window panes.

Talking of pitch shapes – anything will do for the set of players who have assembled to play. They will all adjust to the field in less than 30 seconds, for perhaps an entire innings may last about 300 seconds, followed by the other team batting for some 300 seconds.

Earlier two innings games were played, but nowadays that is totally out of fashion in the gullies, and a one inning game is played. They play best of five, best of three and all that. Sometime the teams are kept intact or sometimes changed game after game.

Again what is important is irrespective of the field you get, people always find a level playing field to play the game. The field is like market conditions, so whatever the market condition, they will adapt to the market conditions, and make merry.

Offside or Onside fields, restrictions or no restrictions of stroke play, batsman do manage to score the runs, and bowlers do manage to take wickets, and fielders do manage to take catches. Leg before Wicket! That is only an appeal, rarely does anyone get out adjudged LBW. Given the conditions make the most of it – play by the rules, and break them when you feel you can get away with it. Sell what is marketable, provide the best product for your customer.

Implements and Balls

You might wonder that real cricket needs such elaborate equipments – like a shoe, shin guard, knee guard, thigh-pads, abdomen guard, elbow guard, chest guard, helmets and so on. Not to forget the gloves, the bat, stumps with bails, and the ball.

Just two implements are needed a bat and a ball to play gully cricket. The rest of the implements are luxury for such a game. Firstly the ball that is used is never `Season' or the conventional cricket ball. Rubber ball, tennis ball, plastic ball are the types.

This is important for the surface selected, for most of the times, this could be cement concrete, asphalt, or a mix of both with some areas of loose soil. Whatever the surface, it is imperative for a good bounce (say about even half a meter) and the game is on. The surface may be uneven, but again just about meter of consistent area where the ball can be pitched qualifies as a wicket.

The stump could be a wall, a pair of slippers, two stones, three thick canes – plucked out of a tree, a wooden board, or even school bags – piled up one over another. The non-strikers end just has a stone or a stick or again a pair of slippers as the stump. Having two stones is when one has to also appeal for a clean bowled.

The bat apart from being the conventional bat with which cricket is played could be the primitive wooden plank, or some improvised contraption created by the local carpenter. In fact, an implement to wash clothes in the country is like a mini bat and may people use that too to play a game of cricket.

The ball is mostly rubber ball, and sometimes tennis. Depending on the field, if it is completely isolated, a courtyard toward which not any window panes are exposed, then a cork ball may be used, or the conventional cricket ball could be used, but the problem is bounce, and lack of other protection implements that these balls do not find favour.

Important lesson – whatever the conditions, we are all in business!

Rules and Regulation

Call this as interpersonal relations at its best, for politics can separate people, so can religion, and class battles. But cricket is the greatest binding force, so much so that between two neighbouring countries, at times there is cricket diplomacy. The desire amongst the common public is that we were a combined team, we would perhaps remain world champions forever.

Every player is an expert, as a batsman or a bowler, every player is a coach for they know the best. Every decision taken by someone else is always wrong in retrospect because the correct suggestion for the right decision comes in now from the expert, and he wants to voice it even louder because it was not heeded to at the required time, or better still he did not bother to give it at all.

Gully Cricket could re-captioned as Adaptability Cricket – for the basics of the game itself are perhaps rewritten to suit the game, and some of the rules rewritten. It is like an unwritten constitution, and just gets created before the game begins. People almost adhere to these rule books and sometime combine them with cricket rule books.

The first thing clarified – last man batting, or not batting! Then one bounce out or not. Rebound catch allowed. Any height restrictions while bowling, any speed restrictions while bowling, because – fast is a no ball. Current allowed or not allowed, meaning just keeping your feet on the stone and collecting the ball, and if the batsmen is out of the crease is considered as run-out.

There is another rule that says tip-n-run, means that if the ball strikes your bat you have to complete a run, and if you don't you are out!

Most important – if window panes are broken by someone, will all of us contribute or is it the person who broke it. If the ball is lost then who buys a new one – the batsman who hit the shot, or the person who touched the ball the last.

It is like forming an industry association, and they setting rules in their association for memberships and conducting programmes. This is very much like Framing agendas and programmes, drawing up a code of conduct – the rules and regulations to belong to the group.

Two innings games has vanished, and hence no test match style of cricket exists here. Breaks are at conveniences, and there are no fixed times. Thirst is taken as break time, and hence no lunch break or tea-break. Window pane breaks are sometime large breaks that can alter the game. That is the only intrusion in the game that can result in being called off. There is no declaration!

Playing conditions are determined by players determined to play and spend the evening and rarely by the conditions itself. People can be playing the game even in pouring rains. There is nothing called pitch covers that exist. No area is danger area and anybody can step anywhere on the wicket.

A person from the batting side becomes the umpire, and takes over the rules and regulations. Mostly the batting side is sitting behind the square leg area, and serves as the square leg umpire.

Some elders are watching the game from their balconies and sometimes serve as the third umpire, and there can be decision based on popularity support too. Everyone here feels you were plumb, you were outside of the crease – and hence stumped, or run out, and so on.

Since the most popular form of cricket played in this format now is the limited overs cricket, what is typically taken as a format is 12 overs in an open ground. This could get adapted to six to ten overs in a gully format. Obviously there are no Duckworth Lewis rules, for these people are not used to such complicated calculations.

With the advent of IPL and popularity of T20 cricket rising, people in the grassroots have started forming leagues of their own, and have championships within the building where sometime they invite all the members witness the game, followed by snacks or dinner to socialize. This provides the festival atmosphere to cricket.

Local organizations adopt this format as a fund raising as cricket is a great leveler. Every format has its own rules that are sometime stated, sometimes not. As stated earlier there is an unwritten constitution of the way the game will be conducted, and people adhere to it.

Types of games

You may wonder how can be types of games, when already in cricket there are now three types of games – Test, Limited Overs, and T-20. At maximum if you rack your brains you may be able to recollect six a side cricket championship played in Hong Kong or somewhere.

There were earlier two innings cricket played and the overs were unlimited, for everyone got to bat, and almost everyone got to bowl. With about six to eight a side, and a total area the size of a cricket pitch – almost 32 wickets would fall in less than 30 minutes. People who played in such games now wonder in amazement as to how it was possible.

People are so impatient that game could last about two hours maximum. This is not in a t20 format even, but in the gully format of limited overs one innings match, where a target is set, and achieved or defended.

There is a format called as box cricket that has evolved from gully cricket – and has rules where if the ball clears the field without bouncing the batsman is considered out. If you bend your knees while bowling, it is considered as a no ball.

Other formats like single wicket and double wicket championships still exist in local levels and are played like Grand Slam tennis tournaments.

Business too is like gully cricket – people find their universe, maybe local, maybe regional, maybe national, or maybe international. The scale differs, the rules may differ depending on the area or region, but the game goes on – in the rules set by the group of people wanting to play the game of business.

The gully cricket is the best place for spotting talent, for some of the best players come from here, and the myriad of situations they have faced in this format gives them the temperament to hold their nerve in tense situations. The format typically resembles t20 cricket, and no wonder – India is already emerged as a force to reckon with.

Chapter 3

CHANGE IS THE ONLY CONSTANT!

Perhaps the most clichéd term that one must have heard in the last twenty years, since liberalization in India – must be the word Change! It has been so rapid, that adapting to change has been challenging enough that one then has to adopt new practices.

Perhaps, this could be illustrated with an anecdote of a Grandfather, Father, and Grandson watching a game of T-20 in 2011. What the grandson enjoyed as a great game of cricket, was received neutrally by the father, and not so positively by the grandfather. So I decided to look at 2011. 1991, and 1971. A span of 40 years, and the way cricket transformed.

1971 because, India won a Test Match in England under Ajit Wadekar, and somewhere the first one day match was played, but one got to witness some of the best of stars of Test Cricket. One can say that with some amount of conviction because of television.

There surely would have been greater players than the phase that we are talking about, but those great performances were only watched by the crowds in the ground, and then the public at large coming to know of the same through a newspaper report.

One could literally go on a journey – country by country, and look at the essence of the players starting with the then champion side – West Indies; Australia; England; and New Zealand then.

South Africa was a team that emerged around early 90's and hit the headlines with their semi-final spot in their debut world cup in 1991, and the sad exit.

India; Pakistan and Sri Lanka – have emerged as the sub continental challengers and carved a niche for themselves especially in the 21st century.

This is akin to your ability to do business as a corporate. Some teams are like flavour of the season, while others build a team culture over long term. Change is the only constant, and you have to constantly adopt to emerging scenario, but the basic rules are still basic, and one has to keep the approach simple.

The Cricket coaches will still tell you – play into the V, play straight and you will falter less, so in business. Concentrate on the core areas and you will develop the staying power. As you develop in confidence you can look around the field and depending on the situations improvise.

Test Match Cricket and Business Strategy – what are the parallels? It sometimes make me wonder!

Five days, normally 40 wickets for a result. Divided into six sessions -- Morning session, Pre-Lunch session, Post Lunch Session, Pre-Tea session, Post Tea session, Last Session, so in all about 30 sessions. On the fifth day, there is the 20 mandatory overs, perhaps the genesis of T20 cricket.

Earlier Test matches used to be played over six days, with one day of rest after mostly the third day. Many turnaround stories have happened after the rest day, with some part-time bowlers transforming into batsmen, displaying tremendous application and excelling in a department that they were never expected to, thus changing the game for their team.

But with the advent of a continuous five days, games have seldom lasted the full length, so much so that people have started this debate of whether test cricket should be done away with.

This reminds me of the dot com days, when there was a big debate about old economy and new economy companies. Everyone was caught in the herd mentality of embracing the 'e' as in e-commerce, but once the dot com crash happened, there was a realization that plain e-commerce would be a model that works in just a few sectors.

e-commerce was an enablement tool, and the traditional companies had to embrace this as a part of enablement. Brick and mortar was very much needed, click would be an added bonus.

Take the case of Sunil Gavaskar in 1975 World Cup and 1987 World Cup, 30 in 60 overs against England and a quick fire 100 against New Zealand, showed the temperament of adaptability.

Nations today talk of specialists across the formats of the game, and those who can play all the three formats today automatically qualify as greats.

What does the captain have at this disposal as he walks to toss the coin? The eleven players with a particular combination, that has been thought out, on the basis of the surface, the opposition, and the form of players, as key decision making points.

The first factor they say is LUCK! Where does one not need luck? Depending on the conditions, the surface (favourable market conditions) could aid you; or you would have to work hard and bend your back to succeed (Pedigree).

In the case of a corporate, it is the industry segment, and the market segment that perhaps determines their growth. Like an opening batsmen – the company goes to open its foray in the industry and maybe tastes a good success, or has early setbacks.

When it faces the bowlers it is like facing factors like competition, industry forces, and environmental forces and so on. The total that you put up against these forces matters, for the way these forces utilize the wicket or the way you measure up to this and conquer the demons are very important.

Green top assists pace, and hence it is important to play the fast bowlers well, for the ball zips past the bat, and one has to be careful of the edges. A little bit of breeze would assist the seam bowlers for the batsman would be in a dilemma of which way the ball would swing, and hence one has to be careful with that too. A wicket that is crumbling will start to assist spin, and hence one has to play them very carefully.

Taking these as thumb rules, you can use them to defend as well as attack, for your assessment of the market forces (pitch) on the basis of the team you have lets you play your cards on the wicket.

Team composition gets decided on this basis or using what type of bowlers. For you may have batsmen who can pile on the runs, but till you have a penetrative bowler/s, the chance of winning may be slimmer. That provides the balance between the batsmen and bowlers thus making a perfect contest of bat and ball.

As a corporate grows, it needs funds – and this it can attract through internal accruals, bank loans, angel investors, venture capitalists, and/or stock markets.

The money borrowed or debt is like the pressure that a corporate gets on itself, for there has to be a commensurate performance to provide the desired result.

We could call this as the first or second innings (Second and fourth), if we want to draw parallels to having achieved financial closure, how do we shape up performance levels to programme the finances to achieve the targets of the periodic payouts, or the dividends that one needs to provide. There is pressure, but a cool mind and application to the situation is the best way to surmount the challenge.

As the company grows internationally, it seeks collaborations across countries. This is like the partnerships that happen between certain wickets in cricket, for test matches especially are built on the foundation of partnerships.

It is not just a big partnership, but many that make companies grow – as collaborators, partners, subsidiaries, joint ventures are all forms that a game's parallels take.

When it gets to the bowling phase, the concerned batsman (competition), and the strategy that one adopts (field setting) on the basis of expected behavior is the guile on the basis of the captain and the bowler.

The fielders are like the zones and territories. You have to guard against the competitions timing of penetrating those zones and territories, and plug them effectively. The approach changes while batting and bowling.

Situations throw some challenges in terms of contingencies, in terms of uncertainties and shocks. There are strategies for situations, and test match cricket is the biggest challenge – it tests true substance a player has, and true grit a company can show, for they are made to adapt to the emerging scenarios, and survive the long term.

Chapter 4

ONCE UPON A TIME... ONE DAY....

One had five days, or three days to think through a game. There would be twists and turns that one could think through, and chart out adequate response mechanisms.

Emerge a new concept of trying to crunch it in One Day – call it a compression or a Zip file, or it is like taking a hi-res file and perhaps reducing the size to make it of a manageable size and send over email.

Welcome to the world of One Day cricket! That compressed traditional cricket to about 20% of the original, and produces completely different flavours, thrills, suspense, battle of nerves, and most important a finite RESULT, instead of a dreary draw of a test match.

Draw they say is No Result! Then go and ask a team that was having its back to the wall! Perhaps the imminent defeat staring on the face, and the other side on top, going through the chores of completing the game.

The defending team is successful in thwarting the attacking team from achieving victory. The match ends in a draw – an exciting draw, instead of a dreary draw that happens because of maybe pitch conditions, maybe a captains decision to bat on, or maybe insipid bowlers not able to penetrate and get wickets, or various other reasons.

The genesis of one day cricket is perhaps the fourth innings of a test match, when one suddenly can feel as in a fresh lease of life has been injected into the match. There is a target and there are only a finite number of overs within which one has to achieve the target.

A team bowled out in the second innings (third innings of the match) or declaring to set that important course towards victory, such that the fourth innings comprises maybe one day of play where about 90 overs are possible and about 300 runs have to be scored. The excitement being the finiteness to the game, that gives a whole new dimension.

Take this as the essence and carve out a full new game, perhaps that is the understanding of a one day international that I would take out of a test match, apart from the fact that five days were seen as too tedious, and viewers wanted something exciting.

Finiteness was the answer to that expectation of providing something exciting. Limited Overs was what the game started with, and the first three editions of World Cup witnessed 720 deliveries in total, or 60 overs per side. This further got crunched to 600 deliveries or 50 overs per side and has stayed in that form till now.

Over the years the way the game has evolved, initially any target about 200 was considered defendable, that went up to 250 after about 12 years of one day cricket (1987), and that became 275 by 1996, and 300 by 2003,and about 350 by 2010 onwards.

This perhaps can be coincided with the rapid pace of developments and way businesses are trying to leverage to attain more and more and more.

Copy book strokes have been thrown out of the windows, for one gets to see newer shots that may make the purists hang their heads in shame. Paddle sweep, reverse sweep, Lob over the keeper, deliberately played lofted strokes thus taking advantage of the field positions, slog, edges, and so on.

Strokes that would normally be played by a batsman beyond Number five or part time batsmen in test cricket, now became the norm of this new game. A phase of a test match when the bowling side was trying to mop up the so called tail, and the tail wagged with these part time batsmen providing support to a recognized batsman. One got to see some unbelievable partnerships then.

The norm of the game was to get runs anyhow – it didn't matter whether they were byes, leg byes, wide balls, no balls, or even hits and misses. One had to set or chase a target to put runs on the board, or achieve the target.

The game was such that it produced some micro-situations, and suddenly everything seemed instant.

A batsman who would defend and labour for his runs, or was called a steady dependable batsman, was considered a handicap in this format, till teams realized that – chasing a target is like setting sail, and as you reach milestones (ports), you need a good anchor. A good spin bowler who could bamboozle the batsman with his guile and flight was considered a liability.

Quick runs and economic bowling was the norm of the day. This was almost like the Sales & Marketing team taking over when batting, and the CFO taking over when bowling. Corporates look to garnering the best market shares through acquiring as many customers as possible, and reaping the benefits.

When bowling, there is a miserly approach on the bowling side for they would like to concede as few runs as possible, and this is like a corporate department, providing the minimal budgets and expecting maximum results.

Such situations bring out the best in some teams, and then the way the entire game proceeds is like a time-bomb ticking. Visualize the team batting first, and scoring at about a rate of five or six runs, and hoping to reach a particular target.

The challenge is whether they are able to achieve the target as per the forecast or optimize their performance to exceed the target, or for the bowling side to contain them through a better performance.

The other challenge being that of allocating bowlers, because at least five needs to be used in comparison to test cricket, where even two good bowler could do the job for a team and bowl out the opposition. But here there is a `finiteness' on the bowlers too, and they are perhaps like markets, and there are budgets that are set up in the captains mind.

Should a bowler concede beyond a particular number or runs, or prove to be costly. The captain has to think of various permutations and combinations to use his resources like a Industry Captain or a CEO, for the end of the innings is going to the report card.

The typical approach that is taken in the game is very much like q1, q2, q3, q4 – for the first 15 overs are treated as q1. The team starts will all fervour and all guns blazing to reach a planned milestone.

Depending on the performance, the team then decides to either accelerate, or steady the ship, or consolidate on a great start. This is the more sedate phase of the game typically the periods of q2 and q3, and then there is a renewed vigour in the final phase or the q4 for a forecasted target has to be achieved, and everything is measured as per productivity.

Constantly there is this run rate, and when you are chasing the current run rate and required run rate, and perhaps this makes one more goal focused, thus raise performances, because everything here is finite.

Compare this to a test match, and one could declare half an hour beyond the planned time, because a target was not achieved, but this is like putting finiteness into the minds of batsmen who can be artists trying to produce masterpieces, with copybook strokes, elegance, grace and élan.

The operative word is adaptability, and many of the batsmen from the Test teams are able to adapt to the one day format or the finite format, while some excel only in this format, and their ability in the longer version is doubted.

This has given rise to a similar breed of people in the corporate world. Some of them not able to sustain performance in a company, and hence being like rolling stones.

Big 5 surveys of CEO tenures across companies is perhaps a testimony to this fact. Not being able to sustain performances across q1 – q4, and hence the average tenure of a CEO is about 11 months.

It is almost like a full team, and what moves in the corporate world is a full team, for the CEO tends to have some trusted members as part of his team.

That is perhaps the crux of building a one day team too! Six to seven batsmen, and mostly all of them attacking or aggressive, about four bowlers – who can bat a bit too, thus making it a team of almost eleven batsmen. Everyone capable of turning their arm for at least half a dozen overs, so even if eight bowlers bowl, one can have 48 overs.

The crux of the game shifting from specialists to all-rounders, or what can be called as multi tasking. One ought to be versatile in an approach. Unlike test matches, there are no tails here. There is top order batsmen and then lower order batsmen. The difference is the abilities, and finesse.

One of the most important factor being fielding, something that was neglected earlier, but as a skill gets some players into the team, while it serves as a disqualification for others.

Super specialist cricketers were replaced by super specialist one day players, one who could bat well, bowl well and field well, instead of just having one skill. The supers specialist cricketers would form just a minority in the limited overs format.

One good thing One day cricket has done is to make number crunchers out of all of us, for visualizing targets is not just the expanse of the finance and accounting departments any longer.

People in departments have started to relate to such terminologies, and also terms like – I am concerned how we will achieve such a daunting target, has replies like Not to worry, we will treat the last few days as slog overs, and achieve the target at break neck speed.

It has perhaps encouraged mental calculation in most of us, for we do not rely on the calculator to find out what is 10/3, and we surely know it is something greater than 3, but something lesser than 4 that is typically calculating run rates, and also at times of achieving targets to quickly calculate the asking rate in terms of balls and runs.

Surely, One day cricket is not One Day, because it has come to rule your and my life and the way we view cricket. The influence has been such that today we like to even look at a test players score and ask the number of balls he has taken to reach there. The currency of that in a test match has been minutes, and not balls.

Teams today score nearly 300 – 350 runs in a single day of a test match, and immediately, we quip – oh they have been scoring at nearly 4 an over, types. Come to think of the corporate world, who talks of where will you be after three years or five, everyone says where will you be the next year, and no wonder – annual results are given so much importance – that long term progress achieved needs to be justified as increments of annual performances.

Chapter 5

TWENTY SOMETHING!

Call it the Formula 1 Race of cricket, for it is so rapid and brisk, that one feels that one is seeing a horse race or a formula 1 race. Such is the speed, that this really makes one wonder as to how can it possible to play the game at such a pace! This is a transformed version of cricket, call it, a festive occasion, a carnival, or a football match.

The game lasts a shade above three hours, that when tournaments happens, two games are possible one after another. It rains sixes, and fours! Almost every ball is a run. Those who can bowl dot balls are great, and those who can bowl tight and miserly, are greater, and those who can bowl maiden overs are greater.

150 is typically the average score that a team manages in its stipulated twenty overs. Most of the games get decided in the last three overs of the side batting second, because till then this form of the game holds the basic tenet of cricket – a game of glorious uncertainties.

Talking about glorious uncertainties, business may call it as crisis, for uncertainties are things beyond the plan, and sometimes we draw up contingencies to face such scenarios, or sometimes we are reactive to such situations, and tend to perhaps just take things as it comes.

If a test match for a Corporate is about where will we be five years from now, and one day match being what will happen in this year, the game of

Twenty-Twenty is perhaps the simplest parallel to a quarter. All action happens in the quarter itself, and one has to learn to adjust to the pace, and repeat the clichéd statement of Change-Change-Change, for Change is the only constant.

A whole new approach to an old game

If one day match evolved out of a focus on just the final innings, this form of the game evolved from the focus on the last session on the last day of a test match that would comprise of 30 minutes and 20 mandatory overs. The entire game was like repeating the last session twice.

The format adopted being almost like a one day game, but everything here happening in shorter spans, and faster timelines, in comparison to a one day game.

At least five bowlers to be used, and all of them to adopt a miserly approach in terms of runs conceded. In this game, conceding singles are okay, as long as you don't concede the boundaries or sixers.

The role play of batsman is to come and use their shoulders, in short slog and push the ball beyond the boundary, and provide some activity for the cheer leaders. Perhaps at a time, only one steady batsmen is required, rest all are supposed to be firing on all cylinders such that the score surpasses the 150 mark, and that is like getting just pass marks. One can perhaps hope to defend this!

A flying start by one team, just puts in the calculations of the opposition out of sync, and then the affected team has to really think, out of the box to try and claw back their position in the game. This could just a couple of overs where the runs conceded are very less by the bowling side, and pressure is built on the batting side.

This could also be in the form of two to three quick wickets that throws the batting side feel out of place in the game. Two clean hits to the fence, and the batting side would be oozing fresh confidence, thus being ready to get on to the next gear.

These are like day to day occurrences in business, thus is typical of every individual who tends to achieve two positives, and suddenly gets disheartened when a couple of negatives occur.

Maybe one has to develop the qualities of patience, and persistence, to taste success. Momentary success will always be there, but one has to learn to sustain this.

The focus on the end result is of utmost importance, for one should not rejoice on a t20 victory as a destination, it is like a milestone, or winning a rapid fire round. It has only tested your alertness against the opposition at that given instant, and maybe like a game of wrestling, you just got the upper hand, or like a game of boxing, you were able to land the right punch. Some teams get carried away with this as a superiority!

The game is really evolving into adaptations, for there are some new improvised shots, and some new deliveries that are emerging in this form of cricket. Again given the entertaining nature of the game, there are some specialized players who are perhaps able to succeed in the slightly longer version of a 50 overs limited games, and some who are considered not even worth that. But this form of instant cricket may be a passing fad, but seems to enjoy the audience's interest.

So far there have been some few batsmen and bowlers who play all the three forms of cricket with absolute ease. Talent they say is supreme, and so one did get to witness it!

Chapter 6

Indian Premier League

Come April and the roads across most cities in India tend to be empty. These are the two months when film world also decides not to release any major new movie for a nation of a billion would be glued to their TV sets.

There is lots of excitement packed behind these games, for a normal team selection would just be an announcement, and a small report in the next morning newspaper, with some analysis of the team composition – who made it and who did not. What is the strength of the team, and what are the weaknesses. How many batsmen, and how many bowlers.

Capabilities of the batsmen, and bowlers, in terms of openers, middle order batsman, aggressive and so on, while the bowlers would be discussed in terms of who will open the bowling, and who are the spinners. What is the combination that will be adopted, and so on.

Cut to a posh five star hotel in the metropolitan city, where IPL teams locked their horns on selecting their new teams through auctions by bidding for players on offer! There was the manager, the coach, the team owner, and an associate.

Names kept creeping on, and the respective owners made their bids on the basis of their gut feel of the players performance, or at the advice of the coach or manager. Basis of financial resources the team owners had plan to commit, the players (human resources) were being selected accordingly.

This looked like a complete marketplace or a stock market, with team owners having gathered to build a portfolio. The players were something like paintings, or valuable artifacts, and the team owners were like the investors. Every piece was investment was being viewed as prudent or foolish.

The bidding process began, and this was being broadcast live on the satellite channels, and news channels. There was something like a base price that was flashed, and the discussions on amongst the team owners, with the advisors giving their bits to them. The resultant, was an acquisition or a higher bid, and the game went on till the ten team owners finalized their respective outfits, for the performance would determine who would be the best team.

The board of directors of the team (owners) on the basis of their vision decided to pick on the best players to form a team.

The next level was the executive level, a coach, support staff, and the team composition that would allow for 23% import, and 77% indigenization. This was the only differentiation, beyond this the teams functioned as a single unit, and there was a beautiful synergy in terms of achievement.

Teams that focused on the final outcome, and were not bothered by the turbulence that occurred, kept a cool head were the ones to come up trumps.

In today's business world, receptivity to change is a key imperative. The leaders must possess both a mindset and a skill set that enable them to anticipate and master change.

Too often in the past, business professionals have viewed the ability to deal with change as a "coping" response. You weathered or endured change but certainly didn't invite it into your company or business environment!

The healthier viewpoint, in my opinion, is to open the window wide and let the winds of change stir things up. Change is accelerating; it's transforming; and it's affecting every one of us.

Change is an empowering force that has allowed my company and many others to grow in positive new directions. Those changes have been hard for some organizations to grapple with, and as a result, we've seen our competitive field narrow as the strong and agile prevailed over the more narrowly focused.

True to Darwin's theory, natural selection occurs in business, as well as in nature.

Leaders like to surround themselves with individuals who are likewise inspired, and energized by the changing dimensions of the business environment. The constant pulse of change and the challenges and. rich opportunities it brings. The world is a complex kaleidoscope of shifting parts.

Depending on the perspective, you see either advantage or chaos, opportunity or threat: And how you approach the lens is key to competitive success. Change can be daunting at first, especially given the magnitude and pace that confronts us today:

But business leaders need to become accomplished at managing the diversity of issues, problems, and challenges that come in the door. The 'leaders must be able to manage change as adeptly as they manage people, projects, and financial results.

Ours is a competitive business, but competition, like change, is healthy.

From the board room and the cricket field, competition is be motivating, rewarding, and, at times, humbling. We tend to win our fair share, and we lose some, as well, to worthy competitors. But both wins and losses should motivate your team to either continue the streak or turn the tide. The win/loss cycle keeps you balanced.

You pause — briefly! — to celebrate accomplishments and focus on the need to do better the next time around. Just when you think you have the competitive advantage, a good player comes along and knocks you down a peg or two.

In the long view, those strong players who bring something new,to the game do us a favour. Their performance 'makes us realize we have to get better — fast — and reclaim the competitive edge.

Looking at T20 with successful teams across various leagues have been like Catalysts -- adept at anticipating the need for, and leading, productive change. Having displayed the best commitment to human resources these teams are significantly ahead in long-term profitability and financial growth.

In the corporate world growth problems are due to suffocation of the entrepreneurial spirit—innovation is the key to growth. New skills are required to manage effectively in innovation-stimulating environments: power skills, the ability to manage employee participation, and an understanding of how change is managed.

Empowerment is critical to corporate success.

Chapter 7

LEVEL PLAYING FIELD!

Whatever the class you are born as, whether rich or poor, or middle class, or upper middle class, or lower middle class, high net worth individual, or neo rich, or impoverished – all of these have one thing in common – time!

The way people utilize this determines whether they have been able to progress, or stagnate or retard in their lives. Similarly – all players begin with facing an opposition of 11 players with their own strength of 11, and trying to outwit the opponent on the wicket.

The Cricket Pitch – as we have all heard is a battle fought over a central strip of about 22 yards or 20 meters long, and about 10 feet or 3 meters wide. This 60 square meter area becomes the crucial determinant of the fortune of the entire game.

Grass, shorn of grass, hard, soft, expected to crumble, damp, dry and so on may be the different permutation of the wicket. This also depends on the type of the game like a typical T20 game (say 4 hours); a limited overs one day game (say 8 hours) or a five day Test Match (say cumulatively 40 playing hours and 70 hours of rest). The team composition is decided considering factors like playing more batsmen, fast bowlers, seamers, medium pacers, spinners and all-rounders.

A corporate too has similar scenario in terms of what is typically called as PEST analysis. Political Economic Social and Technological, to determine the nature of business, investments, scale of operations, the people required and so on.

Most companies always say that "people are our greatest assets". It is important to realize that people are different from other tangibles assets such as land, money or machinery. People handling becomes crucial for can they be treated like machines in the same mental frame of "measurement and control." Management thinking is skewed in this the thought process of key success factors equated to the tangible world.

As the criticality of the human factor became increasingly apparent, more organizations began in all earnestness to address the human issues. But this was often still done with the same mechanistic frames, which had been applied to the tangible world. HR professionals, long waiting for an opportunity to prove their ability at the game of "measurement and control", also played their part in this.

Of the four Ms of management, three-money, machines and materials – are tangibles. It is, thus, hardly surprising that the same kind of thinking was extended to the fourth M, man. One can have the best facilities, best machines, best processes – but the best is something that people will make it happen, or something that a leader can engineer as a culture.

Similarly a team can employ the best coach – for it is just a matter of money, and train in the best conditions, but when it comes to the game, on a cricket field it gets determined by that 60 sq. meter area's behavior, and the players ability to exploit the same.

It is this human judgment that determines the direction of the game for either side. Approaches get defined, plans are made, and one gets to see planning and implementation happening almost simultaneously. Some proactive and some reactive, resulting in the overall outcome the game will take.

We first examine the surface and the available combinations, and how through the human factor, one team is able to exploit this over the opponent.

Grass The Other Side Is Always Greener

A green top as it is normally referred to as a natural pitch with long green grass and some moisture that tends to favour the bowler over the batsman. The duel become interesting as the unpredictable behaviour of the ball after pitching keeps the batsman guessing.

The toss becomes the luck factor, for whoever wins would want to bowl first, provided you have the strength of good fast bowlers who can exploit the conditions in your favour. There will be a spring in the step of every fielder, and the fast bowlers would be fast enough in their follow through also, for they have to utilize the opportunity to exploit the conditions and get the opposition out. The batsmen would want to do as much delay tactics as possible, to upset the rhythm of the bowlers.

Either side is trying to capitalize on the conditions, one favourable and the other unfavourable. This is like a Corporate that faces favourable market conditions and make the most of it. Comparable to a home grown company and a Multinational battling in the same market.

This can also get reversed with some company having a first mover advantage, providing higher familiarity.

The skill is of the captain in harnessing the right characters for the situation, and deploying them. Not just that, he has to also deploy the right field in terms of slips, gully, cover and what is pre-dominantly an offside field. As the fast bowlers exploit the conditions there is a hope that the batsmen will get those snicks, edges that fly as catches.

It is also important that the selected character (bowler) has to bowl the right line and length, for if that is erratic then the batsmen can make the most of those errors, gain in confidence, and negate the advantage of the team that won the toss. That is snatching away market advantage from the incumbent.

Either side, what is needed the most is Temperament to deal with the situation. It so happens that sometimes the best of batsmen are not able to face the onslaught of some fiery bowling and succumb to the guile of the attack, while comes out one savior, in the batting side itself.

The savior raises the ceiling, and goes on to compile the highest score in his career, while playing the rescue act. The lesson for the recognized batsmen who failed is plain and simple – Application.

These conditions are rarely seen in one day's and t20's, for such a state exists for about an hour or so. Maybe there is an urgency or the deadline is shorter that slam-bang approach helps, or maybe the field placing itself.

How many times do you get to see more than two slips in the shorter formats of the game? The field restrictions make these games different, and hence strokes not considered classic, or mediocre in tests – like lofted shots are a virtue here.

Raw pace, seam, swing, medium pace are the varieties that one could go in for when one looks for the pace departments. The other variation being right arm and left arm and the side of the wicket they would like to bowl – over or round. These could be used as strategy or tactics in terms of situations that a bowler is called on to bowl or the side he is called to bowl and the field that is set.

While fast bowlers maybe right or left arm, it is their speed that provides the variety, but when it comes to spinners, one tends to perhaps get a wider choice -- Off and Leg, right arm and left arm, flat and flighters. Wickets that generally begin to crack, crumble and become dusty are the ones that favour spinners, allowing them to obtain large amounts of traction on the surface and make the ball spin a long way.

This change in the relative difficulties of batting and bowling as the state of the pitch changes during a match is one of the primary strategic considerations that the captain of the team that wins the coin toss will take into account when deciding which team will bat first and can accordingly finalise his decisions. Run feasts can get boring in a Test Match, as the duel is not considered as equal, but is welcome in the shorter versions as it bring about more excitement.

Some External Factors

One day Internationals and T20 has seen the advent of Duckworth Lewis System or Adjusted Targets on interruption that occur on account of some unavoidable factors like Rain, Bad weather, and/or Light conditions, or technical snags that can act in favour or against a team.

These factors bring in a renewed deadline in terms of targets to achieve, a team has to be dismissed before the rain gods start showering their blessings, or before the sun god decides to hide behind the clouds and play hide and seek with the light meters, and so on.

This also serve as a good factor of introspecting for the team that is perhaps affected and approach the game with a resolve and vigour. These conditions in limited overs or T20 format alters the equation that there are as good as new courses that have been set, and the horses have to be adjusted to these courses. Project Management in a corporate mimics this scenario, and sometimes get delayed because of some extraneous reasons, or sometimes have to be re-charted or preponed to get to a newer destination or completion.

There are ways and means of achieving it, for again the team that is determined has the go and succeeds. Self-belief is the most important ingredient and the guts to stay the course despite the numerous challenges that emerge. After you have succeeded, sit back and reminisce, you will be happy that you have been able to apply yourself to the situation and conquer the moment.

The world's a stage and we are all performers on that stage, said Shakespeare, and truly so, an actor is a person who is accepted universally for his abilities, expression, and communicating effectively through gestures.

Cricketers are performers too, and have various challenging stages to perform. A test match, a one day game or a T20 game, and within this the situation may be different. A scenario in a test match where the team has lost three quick wickets, and the pressure on you is to come and stay put, thus not let the situation deteriorate any further.

You may be the bowler who has taken three wickets, and now you should not get complacent, but rip through the other wickets of the opposition. Limited overs contest, or a T20 game, where you are chasing a daunting task, or setting a target, thus trying to weave in partnerships in quick time.

You could be trying to contain the opposition from scoring, or take wickets. These are the characters, but what is the stage, and where is the performance.

Typical pitches

The surface on which a game is played is akin to the market that you do business in. Companies have zones and territories, trying to categorize the markets on the basis of consumption, demand and supply.

Pitches like markets in different parts of the world have different characteristics. The nature of the pitch is like a market that plays a very important role in the actual game: it may have a significant influence on team selection and other aspects.

Like there is a generalization of markets, the exercise here is to also generalize the pitches in terms of Southern Hemisphere (Australia-New Zealand, South Africa, Zimbabwe and Kenya) as one cluster; the Sub-Continent (India, Pakistan, Sri-Lanka, and Bangladesh) along with West Indies as another cluster. The third and final cluster being England and European wickets.

There is a preference for including variety of spinners in the team when playing in the sub-continent as the dry pitches tend to assist such a kind of bowling (especially towards the end phase of a five-day test match, say after three days) whereas an all pace attack is preferred in places like Australia, New Zealand and South Africa (Southern Hemisphere) where the pitches tend to be bouncy. Medium pacers or swing bowlers are expected to do well in English conditions on account of the natural lateral movement the pitch offers.

These perhaps are like markets in business – domestic and export. So a player who does will in domestic markets (home) may not do so well in export markets (overseas), and vice versa. Excellence is achieved by those who can excel in all conditions.

You have had some good spinners from southern hemisphere, while one has seen the emergence of world class fast bowler from the subcontinent, and have and some good pace bowlers from the subcontinent

In Australia, because of the bouncy nature of the wickets, it is considered good for fast bowling. One gets to witness attacking cricket as the batsmen who play attaching shots like pull, hook and cut shots tend to succeed. Most back-foot players tend to do well.

These kinds of bouncy pitches also open up more areas for run-scoring.

The conditions are almost identical in South Africa, but the fast bowlers who can hit the deck hard and swing the ball can do most damage. In New Zealand, the pitches resemble the South African ones, with added wind as the ball swings a lot due to the proximity of most stadiums to the sea and seam and bounce help the fast bowlers.

Swing bowling can be used strategically and depends upon the over head conditions, direction of wind, and cloud cover. Pitches that tend to have more dust cover tend to assist the spinners.

English Conditions

The behaviour of the pitch is as unpredictable as the weather in the region. A typical English pitch comprises Green, swing promoting and humid conditions. The behaviour of the wickets tend to be dependent on the climatic conditions, wherein during the early part of the year, they tend to be quite green, and assist the bowlers more. Later in the summer, the pitches tend to get harder and lose their green. Batsmen can breathe easy, but genuine fast bowlers in the range of (130–150 km/h) can exploit the conditions better, while spinners tend to be less effective in the first half of the season and play their part only in the second half. The humid conditions and little dust makes the grounds ideal place to practice reverse swing with an old ball.

West Indies and Subcontinent Wickets

Spinners always seem to have the upper hand in the subcontinent wickets for they tend to be dusty and crumble after about three days. There are similar conditions in the West Indies. Pitches here generally have no grass, afford little assistance for pace, bounce, or lateral air movement, but create very good turn.

The genuine pacers of yester years with the West Indies have exploited the conditions very well to give an impression that wickets in the Caribbean will tend to assist pace.

The dry and windy conditions usually lend good support to the faster bowlers as well. The heat requires extreme level of fitness & the sweaty clothing doesn't quite shine the ball. Reverse swing, off-spin, leg-spin all is effective for a good player.

The interesting aspect is that the Batsmen can get outwitted physically and psychologically exploiting rough spots resulting from wear and tear on the playing top and cracks from increasing surface dryness as a game progressed, in addition to line, length, and trajectory variations.

Pitches sometimes are flat and considered batting paradises for batsmen in winter; they suit spinners in summer. Therefore fast bowlers generally have to make something happen on their own.

Surfaces are often tailor made to be flat tops or excessively batsmen-friendly, for the sake of maximizing entertainment value, at the expense of all types of bowlers.

Generally dusty and shorn off grass, the rain here also makes it a "sticky wicket". Wickets are flat and doesn't offer much bounce. Bowlers get help under the lights. Spin is the key in these conditions.

Regulatory Authorities and Market Conditions

Rules are rules, and there obviously challenges of governance and transparency required everywhere. But rules are also meant to be broken. What is spirit of the game may be in bad taste for the other.

Spinners bowling a line outside of leg stump, fast bowlers getting to be bodyline, batsmen, sledging, mind games and so on. The authorities' authority is itself diminishing with the advent of the third umpire and now decision review system.

This is like a court passing judgment, and, one going to the next higher court, till you get the decision from the supreme court, you will not be satisfied. This is perhaps backed by video evidence.

So if cricket is a gentleman's game, it obviously must have been referred to because of the test cricket, and those debating the one days, and T20s – clearly reflect that it is a game of the opportunists – for many have come like meteors, and not sustained, while those who have established themselves in the basic format have endured the passage of time.

Chapter 8

DOES MAN AT THE TOP DETERMINE THE TEAM'S DESTINY?

The manager VS leader debates shall keep continuing, for both these existed for centuries, but only came to be known by these terms perhaps a century back.

A whole industry exists for churning out managers as a systematic process of education, but from those managers ones that can become leaders is what matters. Out of these numerous Managers, Leaders differentiate themselves by not just the enterprise, but the ability to sustain the same.

This is similar to a one game wonder that some players are, or akin to hitting one sixer or a boundary, when it matters, versus crafting a half century or a century, or being a finisher, and seeing the side through.

All these are a matter of temperament. Very much like, you can pick a copy book, watch videos of greats, and then get on to the field hoping to replicate what your learnt. What you face there is the most challenging stuff, for are you able to adapt to the situation.

A predicament in business too, for one has cases to look at, and some prior events that perhaps influence your style, but how you deal with the emerging scenario. Words are words, Explanations are explanations, Promises are promises but only performance is reality - Immutable Law of Business!.

Stylish, clumsy, slow and steady, or aggressive or a tail-ender, batsmen are all judged by `averages' as an indicator of performance.

40s may be seen as a good average in tests, 30 something may be seen as good in one days, and 20s may be good enough in the T20 format. The distinction across these three formats being, the staying power in a test match, while the other two formats looks for strike rate. But whatever the yardsticks, aggregate runs matter.

The same may be applied to the bowlers to judge their performances, where in the conventional game number of wickets taken matter, and the strike rate. In the one days and t-20 the economy rate may sometimes takes precedence over wickets, but the importance is obviously the number of wickets taken.

The basics remains the same, so the rules are to stick to the fundamentals. The same is true of business.

One may garner market share, one may be very efficient in operations, one may be a great place to work, one may be the most admired corporations, but corporate tend to be judged on turnover and profits. The turnover is the aggregate and profits are like the strike rate. The team scores, the team takes wickets, while these are happenings and milestones, there is a strategy behind all this. This is fashioned by the leader.

If one does look at cricket in the last 20 years especially, one can surely see a lack of leadership across most nations in cricket, while there have been some great stand alone cases.

Corporate organizations too have witnessed quite a few changes over the last few years in terms of management structure, in terms of response to market on the basis of changing demographics and psychographics. The response has been quite similar to what has happened in cricket.

Expectations for high performance results from customers and the financial markets alike mean that leadership is in increasing demand just as the labour pool evaporates. 'All employees are required to work with their manager and others to set goals and plan their workload—and to apply sound reasoning to make effective decisions and suggest process improvements where appropriate'.

This obvious need for leadership comes at a time when CEO tenure is increasingly measured in months as impatient investors look for substantial results instantly and then constantly.

Enduring organizations are here to stay – their partnership is with the customers. The ones with the strike rate tend to sizzle the markets and catch the fancy of investors, but may not be able to stand the test of time, or there is a change of guard at the top.

Starting with a simple process of a team that has a captain – the leader at the top, followed by some specialist batsmen, bowlers, and pivoted with some all-rounders form the group.

The corporate world has demarcated this as board of directors (executive) and perhaps has function like Corporate Affairs, Finance, Marketing, HR, Administration, Technical, Legal, and so on. This completely depends on the business that is being pursued.

Whether a team or a process-oriented organizations, may think they need fewer bosses, because of the systems and procedures, but one does have to depend on the cadres of *leaderful* people to make their teams and task forces productive.

Vision-Mission-Goals-Objectives-Strategy-Tactics, et al they say. Yes it is very true for that process drives an organization in the right direction. Today's market decrees that an organisation can survive only by consistently demonstrating increasing capacity for such hard-earned virtues as speed, innovation, responsiveness, value, productivity, quality, and teamwork.

The means to achieve such virtues lies in the province of leadership. They include: clarity of direction and priorities; decisiveness; adaptability to changes in technology, customer expectations, and society at large; proficiency of the workforce; and consistency of execution.

Leadership sustains life in an organisation struggling to endure in a cruel market of demanding customers and ruthless competitors.

What ailed India has also hailed India – the quality of leadership. Our complaint was lack of leadership, and that seemed to affect our performances, but we were prudent enough to perhaps discover that it was not leadership alone, but the power of self belief, and once that was built, the nation rose as a super power not just in terms of following, but also in terms of performance.

For an organisation that's wants to be consistently successful, there needs to emerge a good leader who can lead consistently well throughout its ranks. The team at large has to cultivate leadership skills deeply and broadly in the workforce at large so that the whole organisation can amplify, bring to life, and continuously make real the inspired musings of its visionary top leader.

The skills that every individual player bring to the team is so unique, because every individual works and learns differently, there is no universal leadership development panacea. And no one becomes a better leader instantaneously as the result of a singular event or experience, no matter how intense, memorable, or expensive.

To build more leaders and associates from well-meaning people regardless of rank: opportunities to practice leading; assessments; and instructions. These could be in terms of activities like hiking mountaineering, swimming, where ability to lead and skills are developed by supplementing instruction and coaching with actual practice.

Assessments are objective based and out of validated instruments; and subjective, through feedback from colleagues. Instructions are from credible leadership teachers, ideally including respected senior executives.

Like Cricket teams, corporate need to Identify the leadership capabilities needed to accomplish the organisation's business objectives. They may vary from those typically considered standard leadership competencies.

Secure senior management support of and participation in the leadership development process. Getting top managers to put leadership development on their priority agenda and to become involved in the design and delivery of the leadership process —not to talk about leadership theories, but to share their own very personal experiences with leadership challenges in their careers, especially their darkest and lowest moments. If you can't get senior managers to actively participate in the development programme, then it's not important.

Craft a uniquely tailored leadership development programme. That ties in closely with the business needs.

Leadership, like luck, is a secret ingredient in every successful enterprise. Unlike luck, leadership can be cultivated and grown. But it doesn't happen quickly. Given the growing need and the shrinking supply of future leaders, smart business people will give immediate priority to intentionally and programmatically developing leadership skills at all levels of their organisation.

Chapter 9

POSITIONS & POSITIONING VIEW:

PERSPECTIVES AND THE WAY YOU LOOK AT IT

Think of the cricket field like a kaleidoscope. For those watching we are habituated to some multi angle cameras and replays, and the recent helicopter cameras. The perspectives of the fielders are most important for each one of them has a different view of the field and happenings. Their orientations towards the game would be different depending on the positing they are in.

If we divide the field into four equal pieces from the center we have piece 1 that has the slips (in earlier days up to five); gully/ ies (in earlier days up to 2); Third man that are essentially behind the wicket; with point and silly point and cover falling in this zone. Most of the shots to be negotiated are cuts, glides, jabs and drives. The trajectory will be at your face or tricky.

So a company (bowling side) can then gauge its competitor (batting side), and if this area is a weakness for the batsmen, obviously you pack this area in the anticipation that there will be an edge, and this is going to be lapped up.

The piece 2 is the second part of the offside, and includes the positions of extra cover, mid off, and long off. These are essentially areas that have to face the drives of a batsman, or *uppish* and lofted strokes. For these areas, the batsman is perhaps more confident when hitting through the ground, and tentative when he lofts the ball.

This is an area where one needs dependable people guarding for they need to cover a lot of ground. Business will look to having someone dependable and special in this area for perhaps this deals with the competitors comfort zones.

The Piece 3 is the onside area behind the bowler Mid-on, Mid Wicket, and Long On. All these positions are adjustable like focusing from a telescope and can be altered depending on the batsmans tendency to play in this area.

Drives and pulls are the main strokes that the fielders here encounter, and have to throw themselves at the ball sometime, and chase the strokes to the boundary. This again is a comfort zone for many batsmen, and hence the fielding side needs to anticipate a lot and even judge the trajectory.

Piece 4 is the onside area behind the batsmans back comprising the area of legs. Forward short leg, backward short leg, leg slip, leg gully, square leg, fine leg are the positions. Mainly, these again are flicks, hooks, pulls, glances and sweeps where the fielder has to be alert like Piece 1, for the trajectory of the ball could be extremely deceptive.

Miscued shots are also very challenging in this area for all the fielder gets to view is the back of the batsman and perhaps the sound of the bat hitting the ball. Call them the planners, and implementers who have to move on instinct. That split second here or there could mean the difference between a save and a misfield. Most of them throw their body at the ball and block it, and then perhaps take a reaction.

The four Pieces could also be put in a different perspective of 0 – 180 degrees on the right and 0 – 180 degrees on the left. The wicket keeper being on the *0th* degree, the bowler coming into bowl covering about 165 to 180 degrees from right or left; the slip fielders covering about 45 degrees; Point an cover in the balance 45 degrees to form the first 90. Mid-off, Extra cover and Long off occupying the other 90 degrees of the Piece 2;

Taking Piece 3 as the first 90 degrees, we have the mid-on, long on, mid wicket in this area; while the piece four forming the 91st to 180th degree has all the legs included in it.

These are like the markets. Certain batsmen have preference for certain areas and hence strategies are made accordingly. From a pure generalization, fast bowlers normally get majority of their wickets in Piece 1, while spinners may bet most of their wickets in Piece 4. Not that wickets don't fall in the other pieces we have looked upon, but that is the copy book V taught by cricket coaches. When in trouble, keep it basic and play it straight.

When a company also faces some challenges, it perhaps tries to play into its zone of comfort or the cricket V, where it has to gain confidence through the drives, pushes and pulls. Some calculated risks of lofted shots away from the fielders, and keep the wickets intact.

The formula is simple, it needs players who can defend and push the ball into areas that is Piece 2 and 3. This is still considered gospel in any form of cricket to get back. In one days and T20s the straight strokes come into play in times of crisis, and there are the big hits. There are chances that hits to the side could be riskier.

Interesting thing to note about the field placing are the freedom that one has in a test match, and the challenges one faces in limited overs and t20 games. The entire orientation of batting changes, the bowler has to adjust strategy accordingly, and so do the fielders.

Drawing up the battle field, this is like a 150 yards on a diameter square of the wicket, and about a maximum of 180 yards on the straight line wicket to wicket. The distances shall be measured from the centre of the pitch to be used, and what is at the disposal of the captain is the eleven fielders to be adjusted across this area.

When you look at a batsman's wagon wheel of the strokes played, that is where you recognize the finesse of a batsmans class. The ones who are great play long innings and score big runs, strokes all round the wicket. They have a prowess in dealing with any market place instead of showing preference for a particular market place. Sometimes situations dictate a pronounced domination of strokes in one region, and players may also adapt to the situation.

A simple cricket field that has fielding positions specified, but the combination of fitting 11 players across available 30 – 35 positions makes the game alive. This shows the expertise of the team planning, the knowledge of the opposition strengths and weakness (by research) and exploiting those to convert them into advantageous positions (implementing strategy into action).

The exact location of the fielders, in such a way that the ball travels exactly, in the case of a catch or an uppish stroke, are all the beauty of strategy of anticipation, and predictions.

Business throws up such challenges, what is your field setting. Many factors to consider, but knowledge of market place,

Chapter 10

CRICKET AS A THEATRICAL PERFORMANCE ON STAGE!

"All the world's a stage" is the phrase that begins a monologue from William Shakespeare's *As You Like It*, spoken by the melancholy Jaques in Act II Scene vii. The speech compares the world to a stage and life to a play, and catalogues the seven stages of a man's life, sometimes referred to as the seven ages of man: infant, schoolboy, lover, soldier (worker), justice (expert), pantaloon (foolish old man), and second childhood, "sans teeth, sans eyes, sans taste, sans everything". It is one of Shakespeare's most frequently-quoted passages.

Objective is to take you through the seven ages of yours too, as an infant, schoolboy, lover, soldier (worker), justice (expert), pantaloon (foolish old man), and second childhood, "sans teeth, sans eyes, sans taste, sans everything". Your interest across all these stages is obviously CRICKET!

Are there lessons in these, for our objective is to compare this to Corporate world, and see if there are parallels between cricket and corporate. The first similarity is obviously the word TEAM, and the second one is the skill of the players, batsmen, bowlers, wicket keepers, all rounders, pace bowlers, spinners and so on. We do have these characters in the corporate world in terms of specialists, generalists and so on.

Whatever the form of cricket, there is always a strategy, some tactics and focus toward the final outcome. Developing a strategic vision in a corporate world entails What one looks at as developing a strategic vision. This role is perhaps is played by Board of Directors in the Corporate World would be played by the cricket board of the country, region.

Companies consider in the phase of the strategy making and execution process as to what direction path the company should take, and What changes in the company's `product-market–customer-technology' focus would improve its current market position and future prospects?

Like the world has changed in business with technology coming in, manufacturing bases being shifted, outsourcing and off-shoring, rise of the knowledge economy, and so on, has the world of cricket too gone through a metamorphosis!

Top management's (Board) views and conclusions about the company's (teams) direction and the product (players) –customer (opponents) –market (game) –technology (technique) focus constitutes a strategic vision for the company (team).

A strategic vision delineates management's (Board's) aspirations for the business (game), providing a panoramic view of "where we are going" and a convincing rationale for why this makes good business sense for the company.

A strategic vision thus points an organization (Indian Cricket Team) in a particular direction, charts a strategic path for it to follow in preparing for the future, and molds organizational identity (Champions).

A clearly articulated strategic vision communicates management's (Boards) aspirations to stakeholders (a Billion plus population) and helps steer the energies of company personnel (team members) in a common direction.

In short, A Strategic vision is a road map showing the route a company (country / team) intends to take in developing and strengthening its business. It paints a picture of a company's destination and provides a rational for going there.

VALUES

Looking at values that are connected to and reinforce the company's vision, strategy, and operating practices, that companies operate on are:

Entrepreneurial spirit;
Excellent customer service;'
Giving back to the community;
Respect for all people;
Doing the right thing;
Taking care of people;
Building strong relationships, and
Creating shareholder value.

Some of these were displayed not just by the captain, but the team at large – Entrepreneurial spirit and Excellent customers services were the performance and contribution towards the team. Giving back to the community was perhaps the ultimate goal for the Indian team or winning the World Cup. Respect for all people was to take all opponents seriously and not get complacent at any time.

Doing the right things was to believe in oneself and the team, and focus on the strategy and tactics, rather than get mired in the criticism and gossip of a billion! Taking care of people, building strong relationship and Creating shareholder value was all with a focus on the team.

The team was answerable through the Board to the hopes of a billion. Each one a stakeholder in the success!

Values that corporations embody of:
- Discipline,
- Risk taking,
- Quality,
- Customer orientation,
- a results – oriented atmosphere, and
- being a great place to work (belong to)

as a guide to the company's business behavior and pursuit of its "core mission", is no different from what a cricketer has to practice at any level.

What one witnesses on the field is apparent, but what one does not get to see are some unsung heroes who are brilliant performers in the team. This too is perhaps like a Corporate phenomenon of being there, working hard, initiating things to start the turnaround, but not being there at the MOMENT!

Chapter 11

CRICKET AND CORPORATE

The business commander who really wins the battle without fighting because he has done his homework in product planning, market research, or elsewhere may never get full credit for his achievements.

"Nothing succeeds in war except in consequence of a well prepared plan."

Napoleon

If the strategy is correct, the battle is already half won.
But if the execution is inept, the battle is more than half lost.
With many calculations, one can win; with few one cannot.
How much less chance of victory has one who makes none at all!

Sun Tzu -- The Art of War

With the right strategy, the battle is only half won; the strategy succeeds only with professional execution. "It is easy to assemble eleven players, or recruit people in a company, through a process of selection. Anyone can do that, and on the basis, anyone can also do the planning, but it's the execution that the most challenging.

True like the corporate world, maybe there is not so much paperwork required on the field of cricket in terms of planning for many things are real time. Too often, planning is simply a mental process, an idea in our head, which simply looks at the past and adjusts for the future.

Earlier perhaps all this was not articulated so much in cricket, but today there is so much of noise about planning, strategy, execution, mind games, and so on. The plan is nothing but the execution of the strategy.

Problems arise when planning is separated from execution. When you separate the planning function from the execution, you are separating thinking from doing. Which is typical of teams that are great on paper with good amount of stalwart batsmen, and some illustrious bowlers, but coms a cropper on the field.

How interesting it is that good fortune always seems to come to those with a winning plan. "When the plan is working and one is getting the expected results, everything seems to be going well." If the mission had been a success, there would have been no investigation to find the mistakes.

Some leaders are gutsy, and throw everything to the winds to succeed, while some are just plain lucky, for the opponent sometime commit unforced errors or lose the battle of nerves.

Kipling had a few words that can be the simple basis for every plan: I have six honest serving men they taught me all I knew their names were What and When and Where and Why and How and Who. The Corporate man and the Cricket Captain might be planning their answers to these questions:

WHEN? The Timing!
WHERE? The Battleground!
HOW? The Battle!
WHO? The Assignments!
WHY? The Purpose
WHAT? The Purpose

Corporate may be in the habit of setting up goals in terms of long-range goals, annual goals, monthly, weekly, and daily goals. The daily goals take the form of to-do lists. The long-range goals are dream sheets.

Perhaps the same for a cricket captain is to look at sessions as a to do list, and the day as a medium range and the game as a long range. Having done that they focus on the next game, and then perhaps the series.

A simple plan will be understood, and readily translated into action. Successful military and marketing operations require that all elements of the plan be implemented successfully and on schedule. If one is left out or executed badly, then the operation fails.

The company marketing plan sets forth the strategy. The field commander determines the tactics for execution. You can expect to get a lot of help with your plans; more than you really need—or want.

The market is full of surprises which require rapid decisions and operational changes as you drive toward your objective." No strategy works well everywhere. Too often, plans are too rigid. The more quantitatively oriented and sophisticated the planning process becomes, the harder it is to introduce flexible approaches that allow for changes in the situation.

Cricket is a game of glorious uncertainties, and different situations throws up some unlikely, unexpected heroes, and some who rise to the occasion at the right juncture. The important factor at such times is that the basic plan has to allow for flexibility and be adaptable to circumstances.

A plan, like a tree, must have branches—if it is to bear fruit. Every plan should have several branches, and there are eleven individuals in the team. The plan should provide for the next step to follow success or failure.

In war, the abnormal is normal and the uncertainty is certain. So it is in business and cricket. The contingency plan is your preparation for the abnormal. The exercise of doing a contingency plan will give you a lot of insight into your threats and opportunities.

Some of your best ideas may come from the contingency plan. Tactical considerations will influence your strategy. You may need to launch your offensive where a tactical one is possible, not where a strategic one is desirable. After you set your objectives, you must expect to be flexible in the implementation.

Execution of the plan takes place in a constantly changing environment, the rigid plan becomes useless—valued only by its creators who cannot understand why it didn't work.

Strategy is a matter of understanding correctly at every moment a constantly changing situation, and then doing the simplest and most natural thing with energy and determination. Since the ideal strategy is whatever works best, it follows that implementation can create good strategy.

"You do not know how the enemy is disposed? Fight and find out. The decisive attack can only be confidently fixed after some fighting. The tentative attack is not a separate fight, but the beginning of the battle. Launch a formation against the whole front and you learn the shape. The important thing is to get started.

If marketing is taken as a military field general—in terms of deploying forces to capture a tactical advantage. One should put more trust in intuition. The intuition that breeds good strategies and good planning can only come from those who are in touch with the customer.

The winning plan incubates in the warmth of confidence that comes only from one who truly knows the market.

Strategic planning is by its very nature a long-range effort. It follows then that tactical planning is more of a short-range process. The tactical plan is as important as the strategic plan.

It takes the corporate mission down to the lowest operational level. In army, the smallest unit is a single man and his rifle. So with business the smallest unit is the single salesperson and his or her briefcase.

While some flexibility might be required in the strategic plan, utmost flexibility is required in the tactical plan. While you plan with confidence, when the crisis arrives you must pay very careful attention to the worst indicators when implementing your plan.

Strategy-Plan-Implementation-Execution gives rise to what we classify as three types of teams. This is true across local leagues, and may be many other sports, but purely for Cricket and Corporate - The Champions -- The big ones in control; The Challengers -- Those who are forced to play follow the leader or form an alliance; and, The Underdogs -- Too small to be targeted by the major powers but always in danger.

The Champions own the territory, set the rules, and like the hug pound gorilla, sleep anywhere they want. They are as concerned with protecting their position as they are with gaining new ground. When their "strategies" and "weapons" are not good enough to protect their "armies," the Champions lose influence and position.

The battles between the larger competitors in any industry often come to a stalemate. These large competitors are often not affected by the actions of the smaller companies or by the initial competition of new entries into the market. The super powers' first priority is the defense of their position in the market place.

Ownership of the high ground is an advantage that must be constantly protected. When you own the high ground in a market segment, you must establish a propaganda flow that constantly reminds your customers and your competitors -- How Great Your Product (Expertise) Is. (and how smart the customers are when they purchase it).

Your defensive activities directed at the trade are aimed at terrorizing your competitors so that they won't try to invade your product areas. Your best defensive weapons at the high ground are offensive. You must continually keep on the attack.

The Challengers always aim at getting *bigger* so that they don't get smaller. This can be done by knocking off a lot of smaller companies, or showing supremacy on the weaker teams. It should never be attempted by attacking the major powers.

The Challengers are in the extremely vulnerable middle ground. They can be affected by the actions of the super powers, and are the targets of the business guerrilla as he tries to grow.

A study of the evolution of many industries shows an interesting and rather frightening phenomenon. In the initial stages of development of a new industry, we often see a rather normal distribution of share between large, medium-sized, and small companies.

As the industry moves into maturity, the medium-sized companies disappear and the market is shaped around the giants at one extreme and the guerrillas at another. The never-never land where you never-never want to be is the medium sized company in the secondary position in a market.

The Underdogs with a small market share -- Dreaming for a miracle, and Struggling for survival. While the territory of these small companies may appear to be secure, it always depends on the activities of some super power. And when this Underdog wakes up he often takes whatever he chooses from the marketplace. As each industry matures, the pattern is repeated and the ripple effects go on and on

The Battle In every industry:
On the defense are the industry leaders,
On the offensive are the secondary companies,
And Fighting like guerrillas are dozens of other smaller companies.

Every industry is its own marketing world:

In the real world:
1. The Champions occupy the high ground.
2. The secondary powers take what they can get.
3. The guerrillas are at the beachheads.

—and when the super power moves, there is a ripple effect which affects everyone else.

The next time you watch a game of cricket, remember – it's not just a game, but a field where corporate strategies are being planned and executed live.